Art Without Description:
In Puncto Reflexionis

Ryan Steinbeck is the author of eleven previous collections of poetry:

Art Without Description: Ab Initio	2019
Soul Ownership	2016
Winter Solstice And What Follows -	2014
Sets In The West -	2014
Rises In The East -	2014
Tales Of A Stone Mason -	2013
Inside The Heart -	2011
One House Left Standing -	2009
Hurricane Catherine -	2007
Upper Level Disturbance -	2005
From Darkness Into Light -	2004

Art Without Description:
In Puncto Reflexionis

Ryan Fredric Steinbeck

Edited by Shepherd Editing
Cover Painting by Conner Smenyak
Cover creation by Michael R. Steinbeck

Published by Ryan Fredric Steinbeck
2021

Copyright © 2021 by Ryan Fredric Steinbeck
All rights reserved. This book or any portion thereof may not be reproduced or used in any manner whatsoever without the express written permission of the publisher except for the use of brief quotations in a book review or scholarly journal.

ISBN: 978-0-578-24616-1
Steinbeck Publications
Chesterton, Indiana 46304
First Printing 2021
Publication Date: March 26th, 2021

Ordering Information:

Special discounts are available on quantity purchases by corporations, associations, educators, and others. For details, contact the publisher.
U.S. trade bookstores and wholesalers: Please contact Ryan Fredric Steinbeck: email **ryan@ryanfsteinbeck.com**

Dedications

For Robin Snyder.

Contents

ALL THAT WAS ANYTHING 1

HESITATION 2

MEMORY AND HABIT OF A MOTH 3

GET UNTANGLED 4

A CHANCE MEETING WITH AN EX IN MY HEAD 5

ON HEARING ABOUT YOU 6

SHE 7

FOR ONCE 8

I DON'T FEEL ANYTHING 9

LOYALTY 10

SNAPSHOT 11

PHANTOM 12

CAUSATUM 13

BECAUSE YOU HAD CLOUDS 14

IMPOSSIBILITY 16

MOVE ON 17

AMERICAN PRAYER 19

ANIMALS IN CAGES 20

IDENTITY WHORE 21

QUE PASO'?	22
MASON JARS AND SKINNY JEANS	23
SAVVY	24
SMUG	25
FRIENDS WITH DICTATORS	26
IGNORANCE BUS	27
THE BEST THERE EVER WAS	28
RIGHT SIDE OF THE ROAD	29
BELLWETHER	30
FIVE FATHOM HOLE	32
RUNAWAY TRAIN	34
UNHEALED	35
THE KING OF NO REPLY	36
NON ZERO SUM GAME	37
TGU	38
VANTAGE POINT	39
OVER ANALYSIS	41
CLAMORING FOR COMPLIMENTS	43
THE HIDDEN HAND	45
CONTRADICTIONS AND COWARDICE	46
TRUTH AND GOODNESS	47

TRUTH IN THE HEART	48
AN IDEA	49
IN MY MIND	50
KEEP GOING	51
FORGIVENESS	52
ALIVE	54
PRAJÑA	55
RISE	56

Acknowledgements:

Thanks to Cindy. Michael R Steinbeck, Connor and Sarah Smenyak. I would like to thank my teachers, mentors, friends and of course my family.

Alla Prima (Who We Were)

All That Was Anything

The tallest structure on the highest ground,
crumbles to the dusty earth bed,
once towering over everything,
it has always deviated from convention,
it has always been destined to fail.
Alterations, inferior materials,
death of authority,
circumstances leading to destruction of commonality.
Monuments of deviation,
redesigned to differentiate,
now moving in a figurative, diagonal line,
no longer a straight answer.
We watch as the sun goes out,
as the anatomy of our compatibility is distorted.
We gather resources to segment off the good and bad,
based on tolerance and empirical philosophy.
We dislodge ourselves from theory.
All that was anything has changed permanently,
repeatedly denying nature and nurture,
ignoring causeways and temples of stature,
eyes focused at the back of our heads, fearing rapture,
as we rebuild the ruins of hope for the future.

Hesitation

Head to the ground,
feeling the earth's pulse,
this is my worship.

Balance between the outside and the in,
still like a stone,
endure the confines of mayhem.

Breathe in and out,
awakening, numbing,
the harshness of the day cannot penetrate.

Hesitation,
holding on for a final moment,
just before it begins,
before I let it all in.

Memory And Habit Of A Moth

With her little feet,
she clings on tight,
to a quiet balcony five stories up.
Wings spread wide,
she stays the night on the patio glass,
still warm from the reign of the beating sun.

Come morning she remains,
as she stretches and flaps her wings,
then off on her own again.
I don't know where she goes,
but by memory and habit,
she returns to precisely the same spot.
I'm a spectator of this routine.
Day to night, night to day,
she does it the same.
I thank her for the intrigue,
for keeping me company.

Get Untangled

Our collage of cut out phrases on a wall,
my favorite was "Get Untangled."
Years in the making,
a humorous, nostalgic reminder,
of the naivety of childhood,
the understanding of remembering,
the pieces existing that make up the whole,
even when, individually, they are incomplete,
that we'd not be where or who we are without them.

I believe in resolve,
but I'm not naïve to its shortcomings.
I know there is always good and bad compiled together,
like the collage we created,
the upbringing we experienced.
I cannot separate them,
or choose what's worth keeping or what's worth disposing.
All of it is who I am,
all of it I cherish,
I cannot get untangled from any of it,
nor would I ever wish to.

A Chance Meeting With An Ex In My Head

Years later, a chance meeting,
we convene over coffee.
You look happy,
you took his name,
you didn't take mine.
The alarm bells sounded,
I turned a blind eye all the same,
I'm a huge fan of blame.
A promised land on layaway,
until we declared emotional bankruptcy,
now a photograph covering a hole in a wall.
A constellation of circumstances we couldn't control.
I loved the idea of not having a pursuit,
yet I was always following your lead.
You mentioned matrimony,
you bought a dress,
we were victims of separation distress.
In the end you said you never loved me,
at the start you said "I love you" first.

It wasn't easy,
but you dove in, so I did too,
soon to realize you were over your head,
you wanted to be somewhere else.
I went from an intruder in my own house,
to the odd one out.
I'm not here to announce a love recurred,
I simply woke with memories stirred,
and today I just wanted the last word.

On Hearing About You

Meandering eyes,
set on the misery of storm clouds,
wild horses racing to obsidian darkness.

I haven't forgotten,
my cautionary vision,
reflecting my hopes and resentments,
against my own alternatives.
I excel at smug oversights,
and cowardly silhouettes,
the shape of who I want to be to you haunts me.

With a reflection indecipherable,
from overcast memories,
I contour and contort,
with every clemency.
You preach as a friend,
that regret is an inoperable disease.

This audial event as is,
I've said it,
done it,
it's here now
I can no longer run from it.

You're an embedded memory,
a welcomed illness,
I can't catch it,
but I'm not immune,
this happens every time,
when hearing about you.

She

Sometimes shadow,
sometimes, sunlight,
sometimes docked at sea,
oftentimes, sinking.

A compass spinning,
vibrations in steerage,
to a great unknown.
Always determined,
never directed,
a mind at war with lucidity.

With expectations at unreachable heights,
she'd be unable to attain them herself,
if the tables were to turn.
Her sketches display contradictions,
both beautiful and bitter.

She seeks a guiding light,
through a maze of fear inside,
if only she could see herself as I do,
if only she could set herself free…

What would freedom mean to her?

For Once

I gave away what I had left,
to share remaining minutes,
in the heart I spent years navigating.

Hands of time pulling,
pushing from behind,
I'm often blind to the world turning,
sliding around the curve,
lingering at the lookout,
witness to rising fears in fog,
up from the ocean rocks below.

What's different, what's the same?
What's to be done when effort is futile?
The reason why I left,
solid ground is now trembling.
My reward is hesitation,
my institution is bounteous pallor,
from great heights,
from internal crisis,
from moments tossed away like currency.

I stand, I fall,
I kneel with palms open,
refusing to compromise,
I've failed at almost everything,
but for once I am trying.

I Don't Feel Anything

Another consult with the night,
fire flies in my head won't sleep.
I propose a change,
after time's been stalking me.
I'm not exempt from inevitability,
I just don't feel anything.

Once upon a time,
winters and summers had sentiment.
In the age of worry and sorrow,
happiness was change,
nothing hinged on absolute,
my dissidence cast deep in caverns,
my spirits now buried in the avalanche.

I attempt to make up for failures,
to overfill the fullness of the moment,
but the feebleness of the mind when defeated,
is difficult to draw back in.
I still laugh, smile, cry,
at a chord change, a movie line, even a memory,
but it's often selfish pity,
a toe in the water,
meaningless in the palace of emotion and compromise.

I'd love to have a fondness for sentimentality,
or a heartache for the loss of integrity,
but that's just too much magnanimity,
when I don't feel anything.

Loyalty

Loyalty is a decision,
in rooms without windows,
doors without handles,
dark tunnels convincing light it's pointless.
Loyalty keeps you championing a friend,
despite all evidence against.
It can derail a passage,
assuring you wrong is right,
keep you in a losing fight,
make you victim and perpetrator of the same crime.

Loyalty deceives at the breakpoint,
common sense rarely intervenes,
as those you love,
see the monster you've become,
suffer from what you've done.

If you lose the constraints,
that weren't actually keeping you in place,
your vision will clear
you can tell your story,
clean your slate,
pick up the pieces,
start over again.

Snapshot

The whirlwind story circulates,
I'm the next to be demonized.
What I believed to be faith,
didn't keep the devil away.

By the time I arrived,
cobwebs redecorated my attic,
I rattled around this verse,
hoping for a blessing,
to end this curse.

Abundance of empathy,
no sympathy for this devil,
I stoop to that level,
to criticize first.
When I feel dissention,
the old man is a history lesson,
a roadmap to circumvent repercussions.

They illuminated every corner of my story,
mercilessly, relentlessly determined.
A lifetime of honor,
with one single indiscretion.
A cautionary tale is all they'll see,
a snapshot is all I'll ever be.

Phantom

Morning transfiguration,
possesses me,
love and desire comply.
A myriad of scars,
a higher elevation,
the minds of saints and sinners are the same.
Sound the alarm,
round up the troops,
push me into sunlight,
build yourself from shadows,
in pastures where you cried wolf,
we see through you,
fantasies materialize from fear,
diseases from a cure,
you're a phantom of who you were.

Causatum

Once upon a time
on a cold night in the suburbs,
it enters through the faulty plumbing,
finding its way into the water supply,
then mingles with bacteria,
unifying with contamination particles,
growing in strength,
finding hosts, dispersing strains.

Streams of black memory empty into wells,
where it incarnates.
Weeks later the plant shuts down unexpectedly,
they can't bring it back online,
strange sounds come from the anthracite filter.

Like frightened rats from a fire,
screaming workers scatter with hands overhead,
as it materializes, stands and turns,
growing, strengthening as it breathes in their fear
and turns it to rage.

Nearby residents are unknowing,
the strain is in the blood,
incubating for days,
heading for the brain.

We had years to familiarize,
to plan,
but we ignored and we're not prepared,
now it's too late.

I hear a rattle in the back room,
I feel a presence,
I turn to face the enemy
I look it in the eye before it takes my memory.

Because You Had Clouds

I'm disturbed by the tributary's northern path,
into colder regions,
beyond the Tropic of Cancer.

The sum of my knowledge,
the integration of principles
ends when I cannot change my heart,
or warm frozen atmospheres.

The layers of hate are miles deep,
a medieval ice shelf,
one thousand years of pain,
from a book of unspoken verses.

I'm saving dreams for rainy days,
as rainy days pass.
A breath taken, a breath given,
gone in a moment.

I engraved you in my frozen heart,
hands held tight,
flowers fight to stay alive,
unfairness is read its rights.
Brief conversations,
tangled up in sorrow,
while dreaming of a humble life,
with eyes to the skies questioning why.

Light years of darkness,
veiling your celestial elegance.
Because you had clouds,
you constantly settled for rain,
stuck inside your mind,
abandoning shelter.

Hours before sunset,
you seek redemption in twilight,
just because you had clouds,
it won't negate the pardoning sky.
Take your own advice,
believe when others deny,
don't be afraid to rise,
you'll find your truth in time.

Impossibility

I've tried to move on,
but the love for you left with you,
it has yet to return.
I have nothing more to give,
it pains me to try,
this isn't a decision,
nor a conscious effort,
I'm not even certain it's headstrong loyalty,
it may just be an impossibility.

Move On

It's been a decade since I stood here,
it feels like a century's worth of remorse.
I open the familiar gate,
at the edge of this familiar land,
shadows where the wall fell,
draping sunlight on my back.

I walk to the bend in the tree line,
into the overgrown fields,
fleeting are the recollections of standing my ground,
bittersweet joy blurs the anger I can't release.

I turn around to the yard where I played,
to see the sandcastles I destroyed,
a sadness I concealed,
a pain I bestowed,
an outcome I deserved.

The stream runs to the gully,
once an escape,
now a hopeful return to a childhood,
to a pause before the ending.

The sun sets,
the son ages
having fallen on his sword,
one too many times.

A foretelling emerges from bedrock,
I struggle to let love in before it's gone,
all apologies accepted,
now move on.

Ekphrasis (Who We Were)

American Prayer

I turn around for a moment,
for a glance at the border crossing,
the other way around there are guns and cages.

I've made some distance,
but there's no running away,
it's so difficult to stay,
if it looks like acceptance.

With my head on straight,
I'm accused of walking crooked,
with eyes wide open,
I'm accused of being blind.

If any of my innocence was still around,
it's authoritatively gone now,
my smooth edges are gnawed jagged,
my bark is now just a bite.

If I were Saint Peter seeking asylum,
would shade matter today,
would I be turned away?

It shouldn't matter where I come from,
it shouldn't matter what I believe,
it shouldn't matter who I love,
it shouldn't matter that we disagree.

It's not a practice of mine to pray,
but times have changed,
I send one out to America,
hoping it's received.

Animals In Cages

What is freedom,
when we're controlled by a system
that's supposed to work for us?
We're supposed to believe everything is fine
because they tell us so,
as they dangle carrots in front of us,
while our leaders profit off of fear and trust.
We are nothing more than animals in cages,
paid peanuts to their lion's share and lavish lifestyle.

We are free to roam inside the confines,
as long as we don't overstep boundaries,
or we are somehow ungrateful dissidents,
borderline traitors.
Now a compliment is supposed to solve this,
a pat on the head is supposed to ease our restlessness,
it's time to discuss a revolution,
before we lose more skin in the game,
to our elected officials,
who seem to believe this is a competition for celebrity,
not a camaraderie.

Identity Whore

Most of the time it's fine,
learning tricks of the trade,
attempts to legitimize each moment,
like you're procuring clients.
Lack of character is your street corner,
verbal time travel is your brothel,
selling out to kerb crawlers,
direct from a B-movie setting.
Ridden to the point of mimicry,
lack of integrity breeds inconsistency,
one moment you're acting your age,
speaking a hijacked truth,
with dialogue scripted and clichéd,
the next you're stealing phrases from a juvenile tongue.

A picture torn in half,
nothing is real,
your pimp is your obsession with acceptance,
bleeding your ingenuity dry.

Hustling the wave of popularity,
skilled at the inability to close the deal,
you can't overwhelm your fear,
which is an unimaginable inconvenience,
destined to expose the private parts of your hollow core,
as much as you try to deny your true profession,
you're nothing more than an identity whore.

Que Paso'?

When asked "what's up?"
I never know how to answer.
To me, the question prompts a detailed response,
until I get a look suggesting the instigator of the question,
thought it was a step,
then realized it was a cliff,
like bait and switch,
only then do I gather it was rhetorical.

Another time, I tried acting nonchalant,
responding with a "Not much."
Somehow that delivered a boring adage,
I might as well have had a foreign tongue,
or committed iniquities,
for my inability to embroider the conversation.

Adorned by frustration,
there must be an in between,
maybe I turn the tables,
be the one inquiring,
instead of tripping through the answer.

Or maybe I just reply, "The sky, the sun, the clouds.
If you want more than that, then ask a better question."

Mason Jars and Skinny Jeans

I'm fatigued by trivial drama,
Everything has to be overblown,
can we go a moment without you being you,
without charades and sleight of hand?
 Just bring the plane down for a crash,
admit you need the order of disorder.

All dressed up while the kids aren't clean,
mason jars and skinny jeans
dominate the headlines,
on our twenty-four-hour screen,
all of it is breaking news.
How you'd have been higher,
without antipathy's dirty hands on you,
after bathing in the river of reason.

You wear a permanent smile,
while you dream of unbecoming,
of permanently shedding the cocoon of unanimity,
finding the commodious room of freedom,
where nothing hangs on the words you've said.
Then you could take a breath,
rest your head and find yourself,
but would it ever be enough?

Savvy

Savvy is not a bumbling mess,
nor a long tie,
or an exclusive address.
It has nothing to do with financial gain,
or swimming in a swamp you promised to drain,
nor is it a checkered history you refuse to explain.

Abuse of power doesn't make you a star,
savvy is the opposite of everything you are.

Smug

With daggers drawn,
we're splitting hours with counterfeit facts.
a beggar's description,
about a fool's errand,
running low on admiration.

My value,
my time of day,
my words,
all inconsequential,
because I won't change colors for you.

You can rule with a high hand,
making light of every situation.
But promises made of straw,
can only last so long.
I'm still amazed how you can you can walk
to the same tune your entire life.
You are the definition of smug.

Friends With Dictators

Over here is where the window cracked and science escaped.
Over there, a decision to strike was made with haste.
Outside, the beacon wanes,
principles change with the tide,
legislation devised by voices outside.

In this situation,
the worst form of flattery is imitation,
while the fading pulse of a nation,
lies in need of defibrillation.

Blank stares,
hollow words,
promises broken,
liberty's black eyes are weeping.

Give and inch, take an acre,
none of it looks good on paper.
So far beyond moral breakers,
nary a slap on the wrist,
for turning your back,
for betraying friends,
and befriending dictators.

One day it will take it back,
the destroyer will be destroyed,
days will be counted and numbered,
we'll look upon this as lesson lost and learned.

Ignorance Bus

Are you tired of the healthy scent of life?
Get on the ignorance bus.
Upset that females stand beside, not behind?
Guilt over dirty air and water disturbing your soul?
Get on the ignorance bus, it's time to go.

Do you wish your country was one color,
even though it never was?
Do you see platinum visions through rusted eyes?
Are you bored with civilized methods
of population control and negotiation?
The ignorance bus is waiting for you at the station.

Matter over mind,
mistaking sight for blind,
becoming one of us,
you take the foul-tasting medicine every day,
to remain on the ignorance bus,
and now it's ready to take you away.

The Best There Ever Was

Of all the historical artifacts of significance,
there's nothing here to reference.
My preference is always my opinion,
whatever is directly in front of me.

I don't need a history lesson,
nor to read any briefings,
I'm out beyond the buoy,
you've drifted out here with me.

Maybe a navigational hazard,
maybe a safe place for fatuity,
either way, the chord I plucked resonates,
beyond the red moon seascape.

If I prepare and condition you enough,
and stick with my mission statement,
despite the backlash and bullying,
if I stay tuned to the right frequency,
keep my statements buzz-worthy,
in my mind I will always believe,
to you I will always be,
the best there ever was.

Right Side Of The Road

How you think,
what you own,
doesn't mean you can throw stones.
It doesn't make you proprietor over statutes,
nor a dictator over consciousness.
You may be on the right side of the road,
and I on the opposite side.
We're both earthly residents,
both still human from what I can tell.
I've done nothing to you except think differently,
so please take your hate somewhere else,
you won't receive accolades for it around here.

Bellwether

I thought the storm moved south of town,
just as before it found me,
this time as a devil tap dancing on a canopy.
I chose to believe I was in the clear,
this disorder is part of me,
I still remember my place in chaos,
I don't need a bellwether to remind me.

I was beyond this,
my horizons were freshly painted.
Maybe hallucinations become expressions,
maybe it's a review of history,
or a harbinger following me.

I've been standing still for ages,
encumbered by subservience,
I cut myself from every photograph,
I'd blame you but I'm the preferred nemesis.

Rain falls inside,
dead leaves and shrubs around me,
when and what will define me,
maybe I do need a bellwether to remind me.

Waiting For The Sky To Fall

I climb my ivory tower,
into my own anonymity,
claiming I know love,
when I only love myself,

The rain is a curse and blessing,
sustenance as a flood,
once it's had its say,
everything evaporates.

Heavy air full of memory,
distant voices object,
as the filthy industrial sky
keeps the disease close by,
while the superiority complexes metastasize,
until they become inoperable.

We are here full of power,
feeling powerless,
sending signals in distress,
while the watchmen go unwatched,
and the birds and bees take shelter,
sensing a change in weather,
we are all for one, not one for all,
waiting for the sky to fall.

Five Fathom Hole

On my day of departure,
she cautions me to stay,
something how the stars align,
she hears the waves whisper,
 "stay away from Five Fathom Hole."

It didn't resonate as it should,
my ship waits at the harbor,
my obligations outweigh logic,
overshadow my fear.

Through the eastern seaboard fog
the sunset battles cold,
leaving Deadmans Harbour,
I glance a darkness where the sky caresses water.

Conscience is a premonition,
predictions become prophecy,
The darkness kisses the horizon,
then vanishes before me,
I didn't pay it any mind,
I've witnessed light plays tricks that way.

Maybe my sins have come to fruition,
maybe it was ineffable,
too many aired grievances with the sea,
luck never outweighs the balance of things.

Somewhere the earth shifts,
the compass plays tricks,
by an ironic twist of fate,
I find myself at Five Fathom Hole,
whatever was lurking among shadows,
 is bearing down on me now.

My boat drifts astern under the bows of the barge,
the bonaventure mast strikes the hawser,
as water churns over me,
spilling me into the sea,
the mizzenmast and topcastle collapse,
the tentacles of waves pull the boat under,
ending my chapter in this story.

When news breaks tomorrow,
you'll say "I told you so,"
you'll mourn me as an open water casualty.
It must be stored electrical impulses,
I see my bones descending to the bed of the harbor,
a mile from Grindstone Island.

One day the currents may forgive me,
or the lighthouse keeper will discover me.
Until then it's my destiny,
by the last kiss of gravity,
I guess I'm where I was always meant to be,
laid to rest at the bottom of the sea.

Runaway Train

Every morning it feels like my life has just begun,
as if I hadn't existed before.
I wonder how I've gotten here:
the choices,
the lack of choices,
the procrastination.

Life is a runaway train,
make sure you have a window seat.

Unhealed

I'm racket in a quiet zone,
a seeker after it's already found,
I'm a farmer of ideas in a barren field,
I've never healed.

I'm the reason there's no reason to reason with me,
the reason there's no change in scenery,
I'm the difference between what's wrong
and what could never be,
I've never healed.

Shine a light on my failures,
disparage my process,
find a new way to make me look a fool,
I hope it's worth it.
When your motive is revealed,
you'll understand there's nothing left to hurt me,
I've never healed.

The King Of No Reply

You're no longer judge and jury,
I've extended beyond condemnation,
it isn't a surreptitious decision,
yours is a caricature of the character I've become.

Once off the cuff in reply,
now an expert in silence,
the antagonist to your prophecy.
Mine is not malfeasance,
I endured a maelstrom on my own,
winnowed the crowded headspace,
until I cut the deadwood from my life.

I cannot be quelled anymore,
the textiles of our past are worn,
your subjugation in this story,
migrated to another mind,
my watershed event cannot be reversed,
still, silence doesn't always equate to apathy,
I needed my pain to get here,
just because it's not the path you endorse,
doesn't mean I've gone awry,
it's not war if it's only waged on one side,
I'm the king of no reply.

Non Zero Sum Game

You're a tough sell,
but love isn't product placement.
a scrum leaves your heart on the pavement,
emotional casings scattered at your feet.

So you fail once or twice,
dry your eyes,
exhume your heart from the gravesite,
love isn't lost and found,
you can't intersplice your feelings,
then flood the airwaves pleading for support,
after there's no one left to come around.

The search can be futile,
demand requires supply,
until you rise to the occasion,
willing to give as much as you take,
it will continue this way,
love is a non-zero-sum game.

TGU

I'm intrigued by the unknown,
some mysteries should be left alone,
like a story with no beginning
I don't want to know where my route ends.

If this was the last day?
What would I do?
What would I say?
Who would I say it to?
What about you?

Vantage Point

We're looking at the same view,
from two different vantage points,
reaching vastly different conclusions.
Maybe if we bridge the gap,
meet half way, switch places for a moment,
we might gain some appreciation for the bigger picture,
one that paints all of us as peaceful equals.

Craquelure (What We Will Become)

Over Analysis

I crossed paths with a psychiatrist at a party,
in the only room without laughter and noise,
we both wanted an escape.
Apparently for her there are no days' off,
she immediately knew I was troubled,
asking if I'd share.

I said, "Doc, this poetry is supposed to write itself,
but I'm not sure I have the melancholy to continue.
I think I've lost my brooding mojo,
I try to write about sadness when I have little,
I'm supposed to be able to mourn at will,
lying like that used to be a skill.

"Simplicity," she said, "from beginning to end.
Your make believe is your reality, but also pretend.
To be a part of pain, you have to be removed from it.
To be a part of the world, it has to be part of you.
If the 'why' changes, then change the 'because.'
You can't continually try to solve the same problem."

"I know," I said. "I've forced love, happiness, anger, and regret
to the point where they're all filing complaints.
I focus on third, and put first person in a cage."

"Instead of bypassing, try a direct route.
Maybe the wheels will gain traction,
and you can smoke the heart of the matter out.
Throw the old palette away and start new,
stop trying to be who you think you should be,
and just be you."

"Thank you, I'll give it a try," I said.
"In return, is there anything I can do for you?"
"Just close the door on your way out,
and look for a bill in the mail, next business day."

Ways Of The Wind

Billowing storm clouds blemish a painting,
portraying a volatile night,
into an uncertain morning,
where kinetic energy rises.
Hell looks to be behind,
whether it remains there or rises again,
depends on the ways of the wind.

Reality is struck in the mouth,
from underground fighting,
with money bet against it,
waiting for the KO.

I've bled for this,
I've taken it,
now I dish it out.
Action is my new bearing,
I never break when I bend,
I don't sit in the cheering section for chance,
I refuse to rely on the ways of the wind.

Clamoring For Compliments

High above, looking down from your pedestal,
clamoring for compliments,
as you immortalize yourself in photographs,
you're not reinventing the wheel, you know.
Addicted to decorated adornments,
sold and bought under the guise of enlightenment,
one day you'll realize the world is wiser.

There may come a day,
when you're forced to eat humble pie,
with your own silver spoon,
if the opportunity presents itself,
please take it.

Next Of Kin

Do I renounce my next of kin condition,
because I strayed from the stable of my birth,
because I killed eternal light,
that shone your favorable side?

Are you angry that I didn't fail,
or that I succeeded?
I made it over what you couldn't get around,
out of what kept you in,
beyond from your before.
It's never been a reflection on who you are,
only a reflection of what I've become.

The Hidden Hand

The mouth will speak,
words will fly,
promises will be made,
with a mind compromised.
The dominant hand will be visible,
beware of the hidden hand.

Contradictions And Cowardice

The early days of my pontificate,
reveal long-standing insecurities,
My alliances, my formidable opponents
all gather in the same room.

I've lost my dictating control.
The precarious direction of my discretions,
shut down city streets,
as my broken oaths broadcast over loudspeakers
divulging my contradictions and cowardice.

The castle of my residence crumbles,
my stronghold is no longer.
My formidable army takes me captive
I go from noble, to sculptor, to soldier to prisoner,
as my kingdom falls to successors.
My confessions to the priests were assiduous,
I'm subjugated by my vanities and pious,
as I abdicate my title and everything I've inherited.
Banished to the Apennines,
I leave the kingdom under my own power,
without love, aristocracy, family, or value,
all of which could've been avoided
had I just chosen to be honest and dignified.

Truth And Goodness

Early evening in sight,
birds in an empty field,
I stand tall above the interstate,
staring down the end of days.
Streetlights pose as torches,
illuminating progressive decline,
the little pink houses for you and me,
are now in foreclosure.

I'm an advocate of truth and goodness,
with eyes closed I feel it everywhere.
In those times I feel indestructible.

Sinkholes to the left and right,
middle ground remains should we choose it.
Admitting the sum is bigger than parts,
is truth and goodness building its case.

Truth In The Heart

I seek the awakened, spiritual heart.
A broken heart becomes a beautiful heart,
open as the sky,
ready to heal,
standing on the shores of the oppressed,
unified with everything.

Time is undeviating,
what you will know you already know,
what you will do you've already done,
dig deep into the earth to find good if you have to,
trust until given a reason not to,
always believe in infinite potential,
there's love all around,
in sight, in touch, in sound,
never let it touch the ground.

An Idea

Your wishes weren't granted,
your hope remains unfulfilled,
your story won't complete itself,
until your thrill of pursuit is gone.
You won't observe forces leaving,
they're crammed into your room of grieving,
there's no space left in your heart.

I have an idea,
stop making love an idea,
stop blaming the wrong choice on the choice,
believe you can find it when you find yourself.
Sterilize the make believe,
this isn't a game and shouldn't be greed,
you'll never love anyone until you know your own heart.

In My Mind

At a candlelight vigil.
Sunday psalms are sunrays,
in the age of healing.
goodwill is reinstated,
all in my mind.

The blood that pays for freedom,
has a photographic memory,
as it flows through recent history.

Insufferable hearts stall on the overpass,
harmony amasses in minds,
searching for the headlights of heaven,
praying for awareness,
under blue skies where rain clouds form.
They can dampen the streets we share,
but our spirits remain dry.

Torches light littoral caves,
promises made to unite,
emerge from the sea of necessity.
The coastline lights up,
from the rising sun of resistance,
from faces of transformation,
drowning out zones of weakness.
If this can't penetrate condemned hearts,
they cannot be penetrated.
Our efforts will not be negated,
I know in my heart and mind it will happen in time.

Keep Going

There will be those who say you can't,
those who say you won't,
those who say you're not strong enough, smart enough,
tall enough, dedicated, disciplined or focused enough.
They don't know what's inside,
only you know of what you're capable,
don't show them, show you,
you only have to prove it to yourself.

Forgiveness

In a deep, dark dungeon,
a silhouette lights a torch of forgiveness,
grabbing my raw wrists,
unlocking my chains.

Out of a hole in the ground,
I'm carried by way of motionless light,
a familiar melody from the tower,
carries through the breeze.

My conscience unguided,
to the entrance unguarded,
flags at half-mast over abandoned posts,
armets in the passage way.

The entrance howls,
wind blows in a musty winding stairwell,
claustrophobic on my skin,
a prison in the making,
arrow slits confirm no one follows.

Torch firelight above,
phantoms of consequence flicker,
dance across stone walls.

Rising above old trails,
paths leading to nowhere,
footstep echoes rattle in my head cage,
through ancient phrases,
discourse on a rise and fall,
to the epitaph of my tombstone,
about a violent ending,
a silent rebirth,
to a broken treatise,
an edict of toleration,
ready for renegotiation.

Resorting to youthful worry,
in the age of nature's reprieve,
this receding skyline tames wild rainbows.
I rise higher in mind and altitude,
fear stumbles as the garret appears,
there are structures still made of stone,
where promises have been etched.

I reach the apex,
sun in the opposite window,
prying into my iris,
her glowing hair, crystal skin,
shines in pale light,
I'm not sure who needed saving,
as I catch her broken eyes in passing darkness,
I realize we're both still seeking forgiveness.

Alive

This is our era,
there's always a way to be happy,
if you're alive that means there's time,
there's no excuse not to alter your energy,
there's no better instance to find yourself.

It won't happen by itself,
no lightning strike will clear a path,
nor will an epiphany light the way,
it's you and only you.
If you're alive then there's a reason not to try.

Prajña

As I watch the rain,
I conceptualize my impermanence,
it awakens a deep realization,
that it's here now.

To embrace the suffering that leads to awakening,
there should be no more waiting.
Face to face at the beginning,
remembering what we'll learn tomorrow,
it's time to light fear of death on fire,
we can marvel as it fills the sky.

I'm cinched on the issue,
not to give in to calvary,
but to unlock the cavalry of compassion,
we've been forced to suppress.
Nothing in nature exists for itself,
maybe that should be our lesson.

The is rain ending,
the stale winds moving out,
old wounds begin their healing,
as oppressors fade into the abyss,
as we relearn to run in the same groove,
we declare obliviousness as archaic.

I don't have a rule
except to live in harmony with all,
and acknowledge reciprocity,
practice generosity.
Maybe then we'll find our way again,
and the end won't be the end.

Rise

Oftentimes we don't know ourselves,
unless we're united with others.
As we gather what we've learned,
from the beginning of time,
so long we've looked through a microscope,
when what we need is a telescope.
So much to see,
we end up missing most,
only the immensity of it all can awaken consciousness,
and only then if we allow it.

We are out here to be found,
to advance beyond expectations,
here I am with a transistor,
and an imagination.

Living through stifling bureaucracy,
revolutionary vigor,
searching schools, factories, churches, and temples,
for the collapse of super powers,
the breaking down of walls,
and the casting of cannons.

When we've made strides, we've made them together,
this future portrait painting,
is like nothing before it.
It's time to make the change, be the change.
What may not feel comfortable now,
will eventually make sense.

In the middle of the night,
we are chronicles of failure and resilience,
heaven and hell,
land and sky,
whenever we become the low,
we always rise,
it's only a matter of time.

www.ingramcontent.com/pod-product-compliance
Lightning Source LLC
Chambersburg PA
CBHW060354050426
42449CB00011B/2984